Weeds or Flowers

by Howard Lee
illustrated by Susan Jaekel

Practice Decodable 86

McGraw Hill Education

Bothell, WA • Chicago, IL • Columbus, OH • New York, NY

MHEonline.com

Send all inquiries to:
McGraw-Hill Education
8787 Orion Place
Columbus, OH 43240

ISBN: 978-0-02-145114-2
MHID: 0-02-145114-1

Printed in China.

8 9 10 11 12 DSS 27 26 25 24 23

Four helpers are in the garden picking weeds. Can you keep a garden weed-free? It can be hard on your knees!

Can you tell a weed from a plant? It can be easy or hard to tell—even adults can get it completely wrong.

See the pretty plant here on this page. It is a tulip. It is not a weed. You might put it in a vase.

See this plant. It is pretty, too. It is purple loosestrife. It grows beside streets. It is a weed. Why?

Purple loosestrife spreads quickly over a field. It completely takes over an area. Good plants die. So purple loosestrife is a weed.

You know this plant. It is a dandelion. In spring, fields of dandelions look very pretty. But then the yellow flower changes.

Dandelion flowers turn to puffballs. Winds blow them away. Ugly leaves are left. The puffballs are seeds. They make even more weeds!

Here is sweet clover. Farmers like it to feed dairy cows. And this clover makes meadows better.

But in your yard, sweet clover is a weed. It keeps the remaining plants from growing.

Gardeners and most kids like sunflowers. Yellow sunflowers might make you happy. You would not call it a weed.

Some farmers plant sunflowers. They sell sunflower seeds.

And some farmers call sunflowers weeds. Why? The yellow flower can wreck cornfields.

Ideas about weeds change. At one time, goldenrod was just a weed. Doctors thought it made humans sneeze. It did not.

Now gardeners complete their gardens with goldenrod. Butterflies like these bright flowers.

It is good to keep weeds out of your garden. And it is good to help your mom and dad.